English 380

Systematic Progression Method
English as a Second Language
the first 380 words

David Clyde Walters, Ed D

Copyrights for this book are held by the author, Dr. David Clyde Walters. Requests for copyright information, permission to copy parts of this book for instructional purposes, or any other inquiry, may be directed to the author at davidclydewalters@gmail.com

ISBN - 0-9762494-0-5

Food

banana  a banana

apple  an apple

two bananas

three apples

to eat

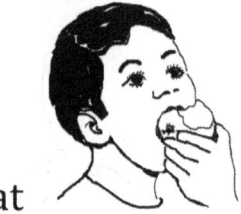

eat

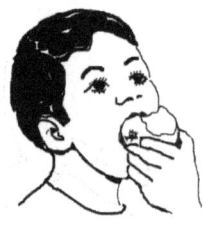

eat an apple

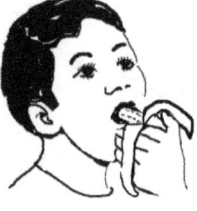

eat a banana

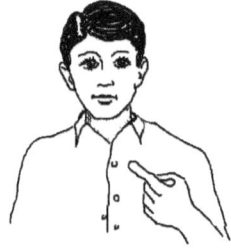

I

I eat a banana.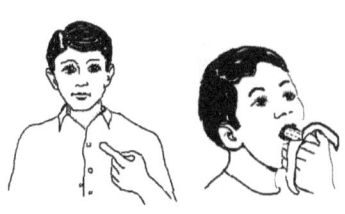

you

You eat a banana.

I eat an apple.

You eat an apple

He eats a banana

she eats bread

		an apple
I	eat	a banana
you	eat	bread
he	eat s	butter
she	eat s	cheese
it	eat s	corn
we	eat	an egg
you	eat	fish
they	eat	food
		fruit
		grain

I eat bread and butter

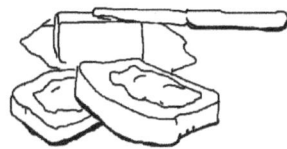

you eat cheese

he eats cheese
she eats cheese

It eats corn.   A pig eats corn.

we

We eat eggs.

you

You eat fish.

You eat food.

We eat fruit.

It eats grain.   A cow eats grain.

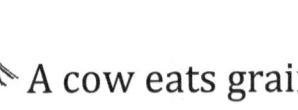

You eat oranges.

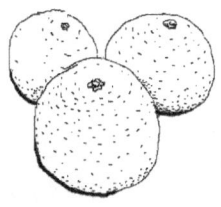

they

They eat apples.

do	I		
do	you		
does	he	eat	a meal
does	she	eat	meat
does	it	eat	oranges
do	we	eat	rice
do	you	eat	sugar
do	they	eat	vegetables
		eat	wheat

Yes     No

 Do you eat a banana?
Yes, I do eat a banana.

 Do you eat an apple?
Yes, I do eat an apple.

 Do you eat bread?

Yes, I do eat bread.

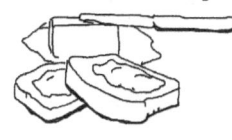 Do you eat bread and butter?

Yes, I do eat bread and butter.

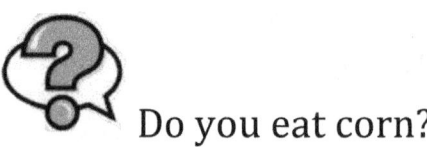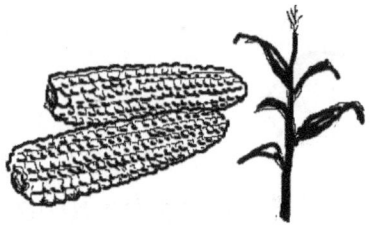 Do you eat corn?
No, I do not eat corn.

 Do you eat eggs?

Yes, I do eat eggs.

Does he eat food?
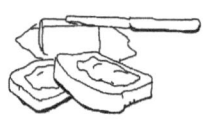
Yes, he does eat food.

Does she eat fruit?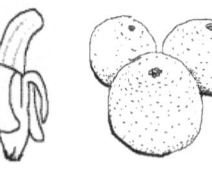
No, she does not eat fruit.

Does the cow eat grain?

Yes, it does eat grain and grass.

Do we eat a meal together?

Yes, we do eat a meal together.
_____
_____
_____
_____

Do they eat meat?
No, they do not eat meat.
They eat rice.

sugar

vegetables

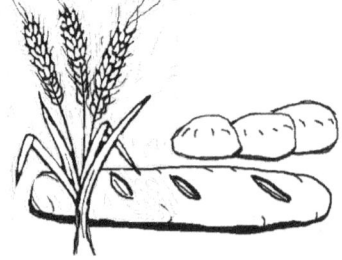

wheat

I eat oranges and rice. You eat sugar and apples. He eats vegetables. She eats wheat bread. Cows eat grass and grain. We eat apples and bananas. You two eat bread and butter and cheese. They eat corn, eggs, and fish. I eat food. You eat fruit. A cow eats grain.

_____

_____

_____

_____

_____

A family  eats a meal.

A dog  eats meat.

We eat oranges. You eat rice. They eat sugar. I eat vegetables and you eat wheat.

_____

_____

_____

to drink

I drink. You drink. He drinks. She drinks. We drink.

I	drink	
you	drink	
he	drink s	coffee
she	drink s	juice
it	drink s	milk
we	drink	tea
you	drink	water
they	drink	

I drink milk. You drink coffee. He drinks juice. We drink water.
You all drink milk. They drink tea.

_____
_____
_____
_____

to do

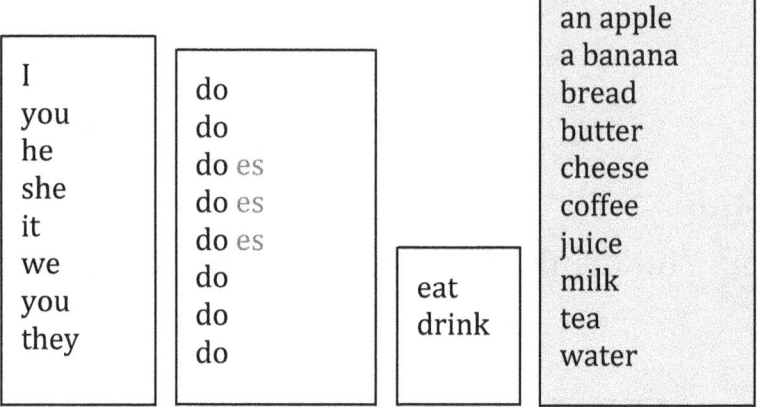

I do eat apples. You do drink coffee. He does eat cheese. We do drink water. You all do eat rice. They do drink juice.

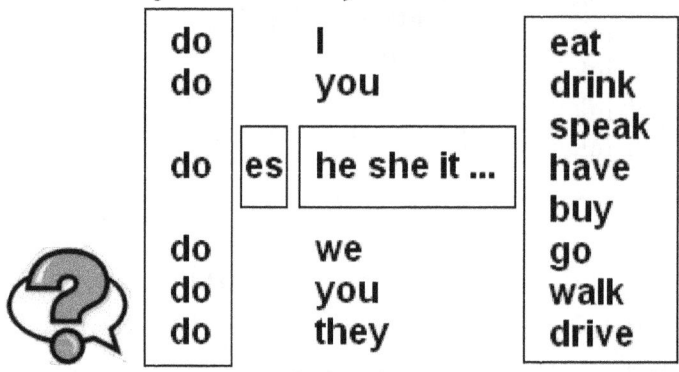

Do you drink coffee?
---No, I do not drink coffee. I drink juice.
Does she drink tea?
--- Yes, she drinks tea.
Do they drink milk? No, they don't drink milk. They only drink water.

to want

I want. You want. She wants. He wants.

We want. They want.

I / you / he / she / it / we / you / they	want / want / want s / want s / want s / want / want / want	fruit / grain / meal / meat / oranges / rice / sugar / vegetables / wheat

I want an apple. You want cheese. It wants grain. We want rice. You want food. They want bread.

Do you want oranges?
--- *Yes, I want oranges.*
Does he want fruit?
--- *No he does not eat fruit. He eats meat.*
Do they want sugar?
--- *No, they do not eat sugar.*
Do they want rice.
--- *Yes they want rice.*

to want to...

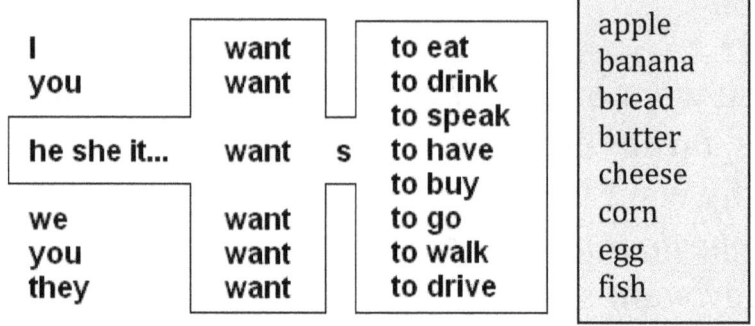

I want to eat bread and butter. You want to eat eggs. A cow wants to eat grain. We want to eat meat. They want to eat vegetables.

Do you want to eat food.
---*Yes I want to eat bread and butter.*
Does He want to eat cheese?
---*Yes, he wants to eat cheese.*
Do you want to eat oranges?
---*Yes, we want to eat fruit.*
Do they want to eat grass?
---*No, they do not want to eat grass. They want to eat food.*

to write

I write words. You write a sentence. She writes a question. A cow does not write. We write and they write.

to buy

I buy fruit. You buy vegetables. She buys rice. We buy food. You buy oranges. They buy meat.

I	buy	food
you	buy	fruit
he	buy s	grain
she	buy s	meal
it	buy s	meat
we	buy	oranges
you	buy	rice
they	buy	sugar
		vegetables
		wheat

to like

I like wheat. You like vegetables. She likes sugar. We like rice. You like oranges. They like meat.

I	like	food
you	like	fruit
he	likes	grain
she	likes	meal
it	likes	meat
we	like	oranges
you	like	rice
they	like	sugar
		vegetables
		wheat

 Do you like vegetables?
--- *No, I do not like vegetables. I like fruit.*
Does he like fish?
---*Yes he likes fish.*
Do you like eggs?
---*Yes, we like eggs.*
Do they like corn?
---*No they do not like corn. They like cheese.*

Possessives

I... my... mine
you... your... yours
he... his... his
she... her... hers
it... its... its
we... our... ours
you... your... yours
they... their... theirs

I like my apple. The apple is mine. You like your food. The food is yours.

car

He likes his car. The white car is his.
We like our fruit.

This .... that
These...those
Here...there

That fruit is ours. They like their oranges. Those oranges are theirs. That car there is mine.

 Do you like my red car?

---*Yes, I like your red car.*

Do you like his blue and yellow airplane?
---*Yes, we like his airplane. We like it.*

_____

_____

_____

_____

_____

to like to...

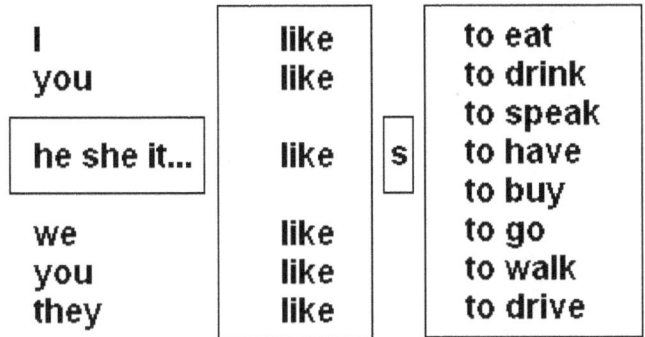

I like to eat bread. You like to eat bananas. He likes to eat vegetables. We like to eat rice. They like to eat oranges.

Do you like to eat meat?
---*No, I do not like to eat meat.*
Does She like to eat grain?
--- *No, a cow likes to eat grain.*
Do you like to eat fruit?
--- *Yes, we like to eat fruit.*
Do they like to eat fish?
---*No, they do not like to eat fish.*

hungry

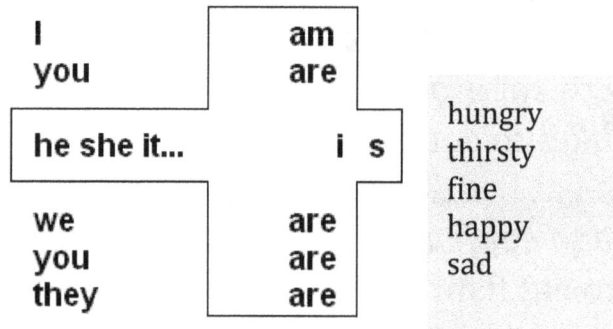

thirsty

to be

I	am	
you	are	
he she it...	is	hungry
we	are	thirsty
you	are	fine
they	are	happy
		sad

I am hungry. I eat a banana. You are thirsty. You drink water. He is hungry. He eats an egg. He is happy. We are thirsty. We drink juice. We are fine. They are hungry. They do not eat food. They are sad.

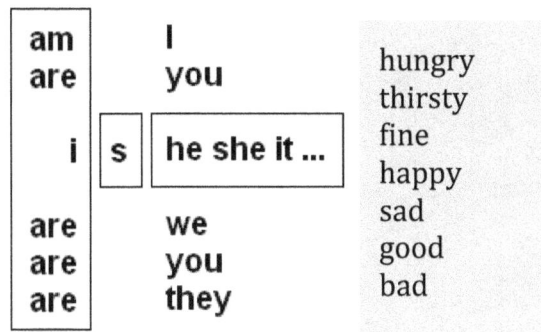

Are you hungry?
---Yes, I am hungry. I want to eat food.
Is he thirsty?
---Yes, he is thirsty. He wants to drink juice.
Are you hungry?
--- No, we are not hungry. We are thirsty.
Are they thirsty?
---Yes, they are hungry and thirsty.

> small.....large
> a little..... a lot
> few..... many
> some....... much ...most
> not very...........very
> any ... almost ..... all
> nothing ... something
> anything

Are you thirsty?
--- *Yes I am thirsty.*
Do you want to drink some juice?
--- *Yes, I do.*
Do you want a little or a lot.
--- *I want a lot, please.*
Is he hungry?
--- *Yes, he is hungry.*
Does he want some meat?
--- *No, he does not want any meat. He does not eat meat.*
Does he want some bread?
--- *Yes, he does want some bread. He likes bread.*
Is the bread good?
--- *Yes, the bread is good. The bread and the cheese are good to eat.*
Is the water good to drink?
--- *Yes, the water is good to drink.*

who?	(I, he, she, they, John...)
what ?	(This, that, these, those, it...)
when ?	(now, then, today, tomorrow...)
where ?	(here, there, at, in, on, under...)
why?	(because, so, so that...)
how ?	(like this, like that, good, fast...)

How are you?
--- *I am fine. Thank you.*
How is he?
--- *He is not fine. He is sad.*
How are you?
--- *We are happy.*

Where is my banana?
--- *Your banana is on the table. Your banana is here.*
Where are they?
--- *They are not here.*
When do we eat?
--- *We eat food at 12:00 noon.*
How old is that banana?
--- *This banana is five days old.*
How old are you?
--- *I am thirty two (32) years old.*
How old is he?
--- *He is nine (9) years old.*
Why do you eat a banana?

--- *I eat a banana because I am hungry.*
Do you eat rice?
--- *Yes I eat rice.*
Why do you eat rice?
--- *I eat rice because I like rice.*
Why do you like rice?
--- *Because it is good food for a meal.*
Do you want to eat something?
--- *Yes, I want to eat anything.*

I ... me
you ... you
he ... him
she ... her
we ... us
you ... you
they ... them

I eat food with you. You eat food with me. She drinks juice with him. He drinks juice with her. We eat cheese with you. You eat meat with us.
They eat rice with us. We eat rice with them.

Past - Present - Future

yesterday....today....tomorrow
did........   ..do........ ..will

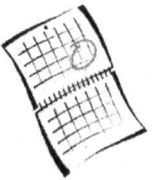

yesterday	today	tomorrow
last night	now	next week
last week		next Monday
last year		in 3 days
3 days ago		after lunch
		this afternoon

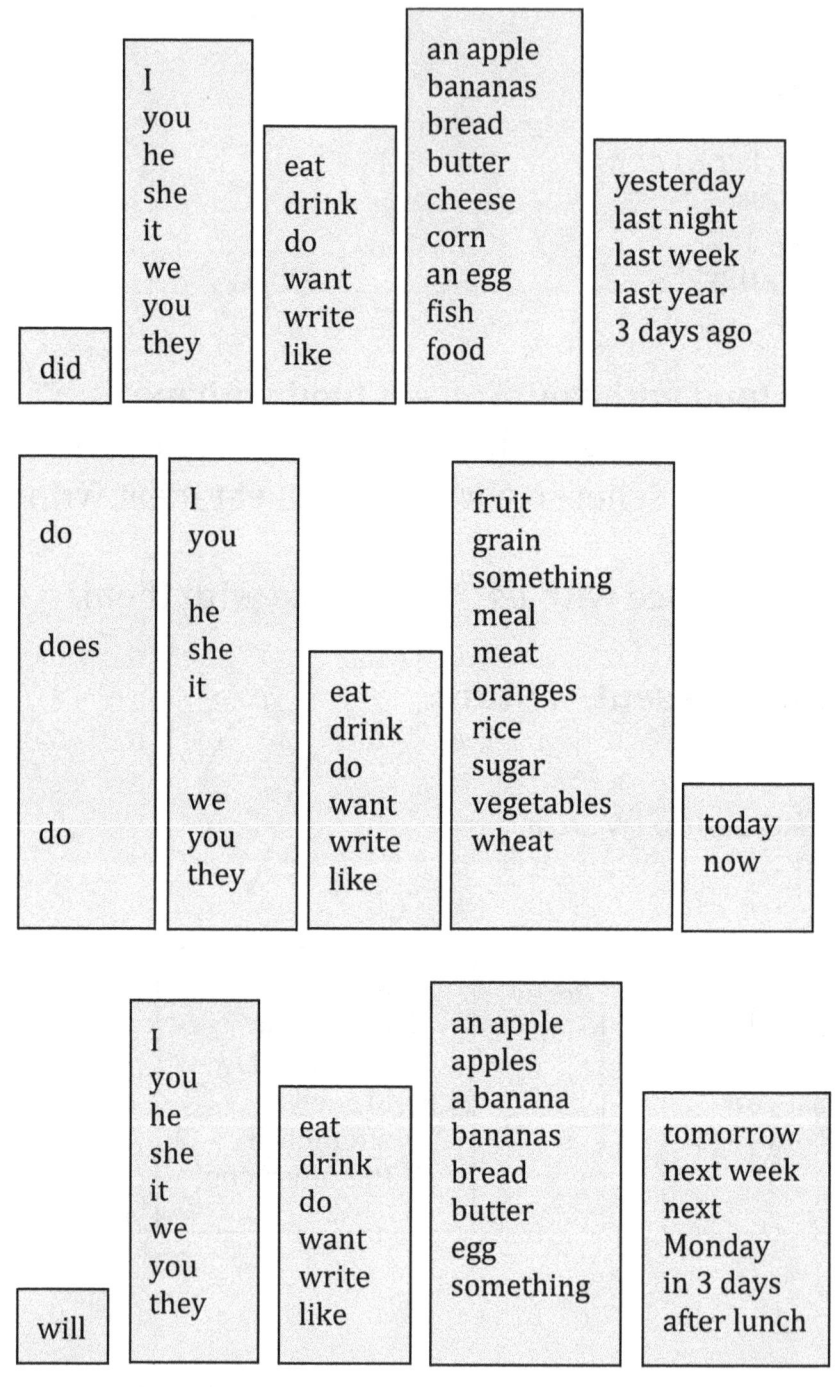

I did eat an apple yesterday. I do eat an apple today. I will eat an apple tomorrow. You did eat rice yesterday. You do eat vegetables today. You will eat fish tomorrow. He did eat corn last week. He does eat bread and butter today. He will eat cheese and rice tomorrow. The cow did eat grain yesterday. It does drink water today. It will eat grass tomorrow. We did want to eat fish yesterday but we do not want to eat fish today, so we will eat fish tomorrow. They did like my bread yesterday. They do like your bread today. They will like her food tomorrow.

Did you eat a banana yesterday?
-- *Yes I did eat a banana yesterday.*
Did he eat rice yesterday?
--- *Yes, he did eat rice yesterday.*
Did you eat any fruit last week?
--- *Yes we did eat some fruit last week.*
Will they eat fish next Friday?
---*Yes they will eat fish on Friday.*

hot - cold
Will it be hot or cold tomorrow?
--- *It will be hot tomorrow.*

Easy Past ... Difficult Past

	easy	difficult	
I you he she it we you they	did eat did drink did want did write did like	ate drank wanted wrote liked	cheese water milk an egg coffee food

I did eat an apple yesterday. I ate an apple yesterday. You did drink milk yesterday. You drank milk yesterday. She did eat an egg this morning. She ate an egg this morning. We did want to eat food but there was nothing to eat. We wanted to eat food but there was nothing to eat. They did eat nothing. They ate nothing. I did speak Spanish in Spain. I spoke Spanish in Spain. You did speak Nepali in Nepal. You spoke Nepali in Nepal. I did like fish before. I liked fish before. I did do my work. I did my work.

Did you like the food?
---*Yes I did like the food. Yes I liked the food.*
Did she eat a banana yesterday?
---*Yes she did eat a banana yesterday.*
She ate a banana?

--- *Yes, she ate a banana.*
Did we eat fruit yesterday?
--- *No, we did not eat fruit yesterday.*
Why did we not eat fruit?
--- *We did not want to eat fruit.*
Did they drink anything?
---*No, they did not drink anything. They drank nothing.*

_____

_____

_____

_____

_____

| yes ✓ | right ✓ | correct ✓ | good ✓ |
| no ✗ | wrong ✗ | not correct ✗ | bad ✗ |

Did you eat rice?
--- *Yes, I did eat rice.   (correct ✓)*
--- *Yes, I ate rice.   (correct ✓)*
xxxx--- *Yes I did ate rice.   (not correct ✗)*
--- *No, I did not eat rice.   (correct ✓)*
xxxx--- *No, I did not ate rice.   (not correct ✗)*

Did you eat fish?
--- *Yes I did eat fish.   (correct ✓)*
--- *Yes, I ate fish.   (correct ✓)*
xxxx--- *Yes I did ate fish,   (not correct ✗)*
--- *No, I did not eat fish.   (correct ✓)*
xxxx--- *No, I did not ate fish.   (not corrects ✗)*

_____

_____

_____

> this.....that
> here...... there
> before .... after

This is my pencil. That is your pencil. My red car is here. Your green car is there. We eat rice before we eat fruit. They drink tea after their meal. This is our food. That is your food. This is my house.

Where is your house?
---*My house is there.*
Did you eat food in your house yesterday?
--- *Yes, we did eat food in our house yesterday. We did eat fish, rice, bread and butter.*
Will you eat fish tomorrow?
---*No we will not eat fish tomorrow. We will eat meat and corn tomorrow.*

to speak

I you he she it we you they	speak speak speaks speak speak speak	**past:** did speak spoke	**future:** will speak

I speak Spanish. You speak German. He speaks Chinese. We speak English. They speak French.

Do you speak Spanish?
--- *Yes, I speak Spanish and Portuguese.*
Does she speak English?
--- *No, she does not speak English.*
Do you speak Nepali?
--- *Yes, we speak Napali.*
Do they speak Nepali also.
--- *Yes, they all do speak Nepali*
Did you speak German with her?
--- *Yes, I did speak it with her.*
You spoke German?
--- *Yes, I spoke German with her.*
Will you speak with him?

--- No, I will not speak with him. He does not speak German. I want to speak with him, but he speaks Italian. Do you want to speak with him. They will not speak with us.
---Why? Do they not like you?
No. They speak Chinese. We speak Japanese. We do not speak Korean and they do not speak French. They speak Russian and French.

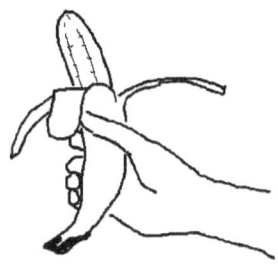

to have

I have a banana. I have a banana in my hand.

I you he she it we you they	have have has have have have	**past:** did have had	**future:** will have

I have a banana. You have an apple. He has a cow. His cow has milk. They have milk and cheese from his cow. We have a dog.

cat

You have a cat. A cat is an animal. A cow is an animal. A cow and horse are animals.
Do you have an animal?
---*Yes, I have a cat.*
Does he have an animal?
---*Yes, he has a dog.*

arm

I have two arms. We all have arms. Do you have an arm?
---*Yes, I have an arm.*

weak .... strong small .... large little .... big short ...... long	too also as well too = also = as well

I have two strong arms. He has strong arms too. His arms are very strong. She has strong arms also. We want strong arms as well. We eat good food for strong arms. They have weak arms. He has weak arms too.

Do you have short arms?
--- *No, I have long arms, my arms are very long.* They have long arms too. My dog has four legs. My cat has four legs also. A cow has four legs. A horse has four legs too.

Many animals have four legs. People have two legs. People have one head. They have two arms and two legs. We have one head. Under our head we have a neck. Then we have two shoulders. From our shoulders we have our two arms. Between our arms we have a chest. Inside our chest we have a heart. Under or below our heart we have our stomach. Below my stomach I have two legs. I have pants on my legs. Below or under my two legs, I have two feet. On my two feet I have two shoes.

banana   a banana   one banana   one yellow banana

 one green banana

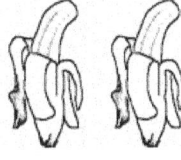 two bananas

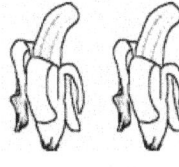 two green bananas

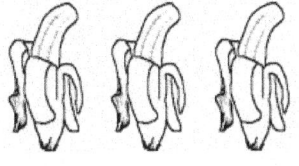 three yellow bananas

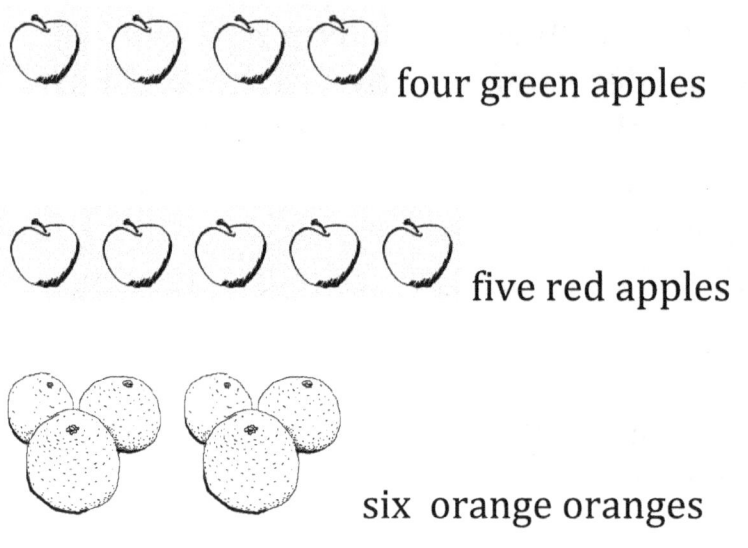

She has seven cats. They have eight cows. He has nine horses. We have ten animals.

baby

We have a baby. Our baby is small. Our baby is weak. She has a little baby.

Does she have a little baby?
--- *Yes, she has a baby, but her baby is not little. She has a big baby.*
They have a big baby also. She has two babies. Her baby eats bananas. Our baby likes to eat apples.
Does your baby like to eat rice?
--- *No, my baby is too small to eat rice. My baby eats fruit, but not rice. My baby does not eat bread or meat.*
My baby only eats bananas or oranges and fruit.

bag

I have a bag. You have a bag. She has a bag.
Do you have a bag for the food?
--- *Yes, we have a bag for all the food.*
Do you want a bag?
---*Yes, thank you, I want a bag. I want to have a bag for my food.*
Do they want a bag for the apples and the bananas?
--- *Yes, they like to have a bag for the fruit.*
Do they want a bag for the rice and the bread?
--- *Yes, they want a bag for the rice, bread, and meat. Thank you.*

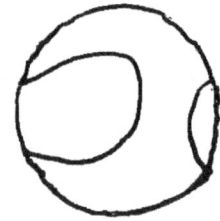

ball

He has a ball. The ball is round.
Do you have a ball?
--- *Yes, I have a good round ball.*
My ball is white. Do you want a ball?
--- *Yes, thank you, I want a ball.*

Children like balls. The boy has one ball. They have three balls. They like to play with a ball.

to play

I	play
you	play
he	plays
she	plays
it	plays
we	play
you	play
they	play

bag
ball
cat
dog
cow
horse

I play with a ball. She plays with her cat. He plays with a ball. It plays with the ball. We play with our dog. They play with a car.
Do you like to play with a ball?
---*Yes, we like to play with a ball. We want to play everyday. They like to play also. They like to play with a little white ball.*
Do they like to play with their dog?
---*Yes, they like to play with their dog. Their dog is a good dog. They like to play with that dog.*
Does she play with her cat?
--- *Yes, she plays with her cat almost everyday.*
Do they ever play with their cat?
---*Yes, they play with their cat. They like their cat. Their cat is white and yellow.*
Does he play with the cow?

---No, the cow does not like to play. The cow likes to eat, but the cow does not like to play.
Does she play with the horse?
--- Yes, she plays with the horse. The horse likes to play. The cow does not like to play, but the horse and the dog like to play. The cow does not like the cat. The cat likes to play with the ball. He does not like the cat to play with the ball.
Does the baby like to play with his food?
--- Yes, the baby likes to play with his food everyday. The baby plays with the fruit too.
Does the baby play with his milk?
--- No, the baby does not play with his milk. The baby drinks his milk. The baby likes the milk. The baby likes to drink the milk.

_____
_____
_____
_____

Past - Present - Future

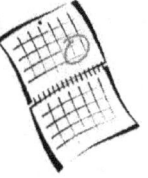

yesterday....today....tomorrow
did........   ..do........ ..will

Did you have an apple yesterday?
--- *Yes, I did have an apple yesterday.*
Did you eat that apple?
--- *Yes, I did eat that apple. I ate the apple.*
Was the apple good?
--- *Yes, the apple was good. The apple was good to eat.*
Did you eat a banana yesterday?
--- *No, I did not eat a banana yesterday. I did eat rice yesterday and I will eat rice tomorrow. I like to eat rice everyday.*
Will you eat fish tomorrow?
--- *Yes, I will eat fish tomorrow too.*
Did he play baseball yesterday?
--- No, he did not play baseball yesterday.
Will you play baseball tomorrow?
--- *Yes, we will play baseball tomorrow. We like to play baseball everyday.*
Does the baby like to play with a ball?
--- *Yes, the baby likes to play with a ball. The dog likes to play with a ball also. My dog likes to play with a small red ball. There is a ball in the bag.*

> in ...... out
> on ...... off
> over ...... under
> inside ...... outside
> beside ...... between

There are two balls in this bag.
Are there two balls in this bag?
---*Yes, there are two small balls in this large bag.*

He has three apples in his bag.
Why does he have three apples in his bag?
--- *He has three small apples in his bag because he likes to eat apples. She has six eggs in her bag.*
Why does she have six eggs in her bag?
---*She has six eggs in her bag because her family likes to eat eggs. They will eat the six eggs tomorrow. They will eat bread, cheese and eggs.*
Will that be a good meal tomorrow?
---*Yes, that will be a good meal of good food.*
I want to eat eggs and cheese tomorrow and I want to drink milk tomorrow. Do you want to eat food with me tomorrow morning?
---*Yes, I want to eat food with you tomorrow morning. I want to eat breakfast with you tomorrow morning.*

bed

Do you have a bed?
---*Yes, I have a good bed.*
Is your bed a large bed or a small bed?
---*My bed is a small bed, but it is a good bed. We have four beds in our house.*
I did have a small bed last year, but now I have a large bed. I like my bed. Do you eat on your bed?
--- *No, I do not eat on my bed. I eat on the table. I do not eat on my bed. I sleep in my bed.*

_____

_____

_____

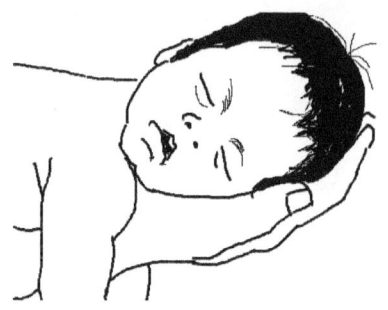

to sleep

I sleep in my bed. You sleep in your good bed. He sleeps in his red bed. She sleeps in her little bed. We sleep in our big bed. They sleep in their good, big, red and white bed.

I	sleep
you	sleep
he	sleeps
she	sleeps
it	sleeps
we	sleep
you	sleep
they	sleep

in bed
tonight
last night
in the morning
tomorrow night

Do you sleep in bed?
---*Yes, I sleep in bed.*
Did you sleep well last night?
--- *Yes, I did sleep well last night.*

Did the baby sleep well last night?
---No, the baby did not sleep well last night.
Does your dog sleep in your house?
--- No, our dog sleeps outside. It does not sleep in our house.
Does the cat sleep on the table?
---No, the cat sleeps under the table. We eat on the table. We do not like the cat to sleep on the table.
Will you sleep well tonight?
--- Yes, I will sleep well tonight in my bed.
Will he sleep in his bed tomorrow night?
--- No, he will go to work tomorrow night.

_____

_____

_____

_____

_____

to go

I	go
you	go
he	goes
she	goes
it	goes
we	go
you	go
they	go

downtown
to school
to work
to the store
to the church
to the bank
in a car
on a bus

I go. You go. He goes. She goes. It goes. We go. You go. They go.

school

store

church

bank

bus

I go downtown. You go to school. He goes to work. She goes to the store. We go to church. You go in a car. They go on the bus.

Do you go to school?
---Yes, I go to school everyday.
Does he go to work?
--- No, he does not go to work. He does not have work. He does not have a job.
Does she go to the store?
---Yes, she goes to the store to buy food. She buys bananas, eggs, bread and cheese.
Does the cow go to school?
--- No, the cow does not go to school.
Does the cow go to the store?
--- No, the cow does not go to the store.
Does the dog go to school?
--- No, the dog does not go to school. The cow does not go to school and the cat does not go to school. They do not go to school. They are animals. Animals do not go to school, or the store or the church or the bank. They sleep and they eat food and they drink water, but they do not buy food at a store.
Do you like to go downtown?
---Yes, we like to go downtown. We like to buy food downtown. We go on the bus and we buy food for our meal. We go everyday to the store.
Do they go to church?
--- Yes, they go to church on Sunday.
Did you go to the store today?
--- No, I did not go to the store today.

Why did you not go to the store today?
--- *I did not go to the store today because I did not have any money.*
Why did you not have any money?
--- *I did not have any money because I did not go to the bank.*
Why didn't you go to the bank?
--- *I forgot to go to the bank. I did not sleep well last night.*
Will you go to the bank tomorrow?
--- *Yes, I will go to the bank and to the store tomorrow.*
What will you buy at the store?
--- *I will buy milk, eggs, cheese, rice, ____, ____, and ____.*
Will you buy any fish?
--- *No, I will not buy any fish tomorrow.*
When will you buy fish?
---*I will buy fish next week.*

to Wait

I	wait
you	wait
he	waits
she	waits
it	waits
we	wait
you	wait
they	wait

for the bus
at the store
in your house
at the church
at the bus stop
at the doctor's office
at the hospital

Do you like to wait for the bus?
--- No, I do not like to wait for the bus.
Did you wait for me at the store yesterday?
--Yes, I did wait for you. Why did you not go to the store?
I forgot to go to the store. Will you wait for me tomorrow?
---Yes, I will wait for you at the store tomorrow.

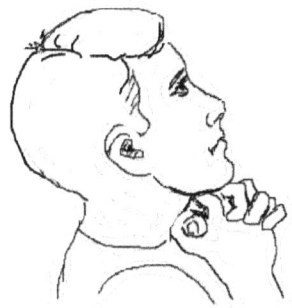

to need

I	need
you	need
he	needs
she	needs
it	needs
we	need
you	need
they	need

to buy
to go
food
money
to eat
to sleep

I need a banana. You need an apple. He needs to eat food. She needs to drink water. We need to buy food at the store. They need to speak to a doctor at the hospital.

Do you need to buy some food?
--- *Yes, I need to buy bread, milk, cheese and rice.*
Does he need to go to the doctor?
--- *No he does not need to go to the doctor. He needs to eat and to sleep.*
Do you need some money?
--- *No, thank you. We have enough money.*

+ to like ++ to want +++ to need

+ to like

++ to want

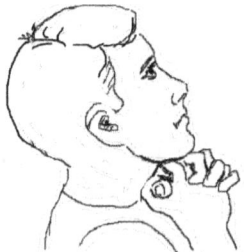

+++ to need

I like bananas. I want to buy a banana. I need money to buy a banana. He likes cows. He wants to buy a cow. He needs more money to buy a cow. He does not have enough money to buy a cow. We want to buy a car, but we need to wait. We do not have enough money to buy a car now. We need to wait until next year. Next year we will buy a car. They want to buy a house. They need more money to buy a house. They will buy a house in two or three years.

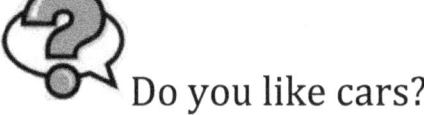Do you like cars?
--- *Yes, I like cars.*
Do you want to buy a car?
--- *Yes, I want to buy a white car, but I do not have enough money to buy a car. I need more money to buy a car.*
Does she like to go to school?
---*No, she does not like to go to school. She does not want to go to school, but she needs to go to school.*
Does he like to wait for the bus?
--- *No, he does not like to wait for the bus. He wants to go now, but he needs to wait for the bus.*
Do you like to drink juice?
--- *Yes, we like to drink juice. We want to drink juice everyday. We need to buy more juice today.*

Do they like to drink juice too?
--- *No, they do not like to drink juice. They like to drink coffee. They want to drink coffee or tea. They need to buy more coffee and more tea.*

Family

In my family, I have a mother and a father. My mother is a woman and my father is a man. In your family, you have a sister and a brother. He has a good family. He has a good mother and a good father in his family. She has a large family. She has four sisters and five brothers. We have a small family. We have a mother, a father, a sister and two brothers. They have six people in their family. They have a cat and a dog in their family also.

Do you have a sister?
--- *Yes, I have a sister and a brother.*
Does he have a wife?
--- *Yes, he has a wife and two children.*
Does she have any children?
--- *Yes, she has one son and two daughters.*
Does she have a husband?
---*Yes, her husband is a good man.*
Does he have a wife?

--- Yes, his wife is a good woman.
Do they have any children?
---Yes, they have three children. One girl and two boys.
Do they have grandparents?
--- No, they do not have any grandparents now.

Clock   **Watch**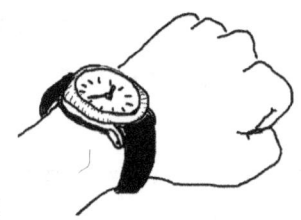

We have a clock. You have a clock. They have a clock. It is ten o'clock. I have a clock on the wall, but I have a watch on my arm.

What time is it?
--- *It is two o'clock.*
Do you have the time?
--- *Yes, it is three o'clock now.*
How much time do we have before we need to go?
--- *We need to go in ten minutes.*

Bird

The bird eats. The bird drinks. He has a bird. I like birds. You like birds too. We have three birds in our house. They do not like birds. He likes red birds. She likes blue birds. The bird is on the house. There is a bird on our car. There is a bird on the cow. The cat wants to eat the bird. The bird does not want the cat to eat him.

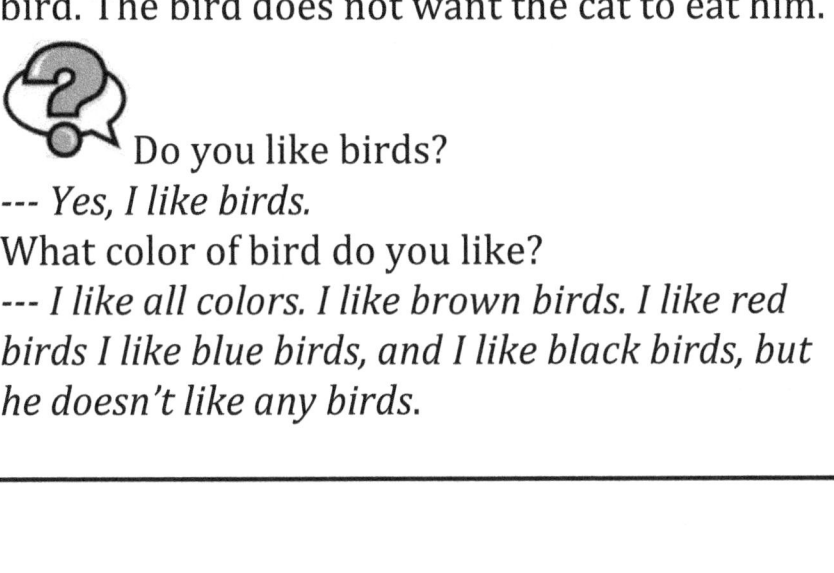Do you like birds?
--- *Yes, I like birds.*
What color of bird do you like?
--- *I like all colors. I like brown birds. I like red birds I like blue birds, and I like black birds, but he doesn't like any birds.*

_____

_____

_____

to see

I see. You see. He sees. She sees. We see. They see.

I see an apple. You see a banana. He sees fruit at the store. She sees a bus. We see cheese at the store. They want to see a cow. I want to see a dog. You see the dog. The dog plays with a ball. The dog sees the ball. The dog goes fast to the ball. The dog wants to eat the ball.

Do you see any fruit in the house?
--- *Yes, I see bananas and oranges.*
Did you see my dog?
--- *No, I did not see your dog. What color is your dog?*
My dog is black. He has a ball. My dog likes to play with the ball.
--- *What color is the ball?*
The ball is red. Did you see the ball?
---*No, I did not see the ball and I did not see the dog, but I will look for the dog. I will look for the ball too.*

_____

_____

_____

_____

_____

_____

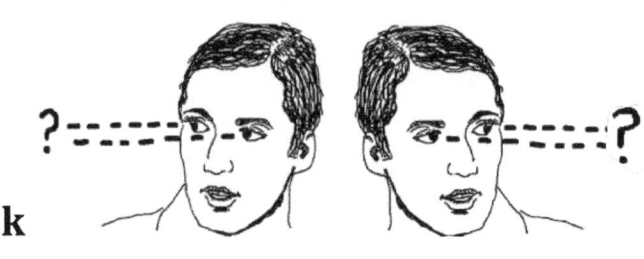

to look

I look. You look. He looks. She looks. We look. They look.

I	look
you	look
he	looks
she	looks
it	looks
we	look
you	look
they	look

for _____
for the bus
for my watch
for my cat
for some money
for some food
for my brother
for a pencil

I look for an apple. You look for a banana. He looks for fruit at the store. She looks for a bus. We look for cheese at the store. They want to look for a cow. I want to look for my dog. I look for my watch. I want my watch. I can not see my watch. Where is my watch?

book

A book. I have a book. I have a black book. I like my book. You have a book too. Your book is red. He has a big book. She has a small book. We have five books in our house. They have ten books in their house. The dog does not have a book. The cow does not have a book. The dog, the cat and the cow do not like books. They are animals. Animals do not have any books. They do not like books.

Do you like books?
--- *Yes, I like books.*
What kind of books do you like?
--- *I like food books. I like books on rice, meat, and corn.*
Do you want to buy a food book?
--- *No, I do not need to buy a food book. I have a food book now. I do not need more food books.*

to Read

I read. You read. He reads. She reads. We read. They read.

I	read
you	read
he	reads
she	reads
John	reads
we	read
you	read
they	read

a book
in your house
at school
everyday
to the children at night
in the afternoon
books at night

I see a book. I like books. I want to read a book. Do you like to read books?
   --- *Yes, I like to read books.*
Do you want to buy a book?

--- Yes, I want to buy a book. I want an easy book.
Do you want to eat a book?
---No, I do not want to eat a book. I want to read a book.
Does he like to read books?
---No, he does not like to read books. He likes to eat and he likes to drink, but he does not like to read.
Does a dog read a book?
--- No, a dog does not read a book. A dog eats meat. A dog plays with a ball, but a dog does not read a book.

_____

_____

_____

_____

_____

_____

city

I like the city. She likes the city. We go to the city. They do not like the city. I wait for a bus in the city. He goes to the bank in the city every day. They go to eat in the city next week.

Do you like this city?
--- *Yes, I like this city.*
Do you go to the bank in the city?
---*No, I do not go to the bank in the city.*
Do you buy food in the city?
--- *Yes, I buy food in the city on Monday.*
Do you eat food in the city?
--- *No, I eat food in my house.*

to ride

I	ride
you	ride
he	rides
she	rides
it	rides
we	ride
you	ride
they	ride

the bus
a bike
a bicycle
my bike
my bicycle
a horse
my horse
a motorcycle
my motorcycle

I ride the bus to the city. You ride a bike to my house. He rides a motorcycle. She rides a horse.

Do you like to ride on the bus?
---*Yes, I like to ride on the bus.*
Does she ride the bus to school?
---*No, she rides her bike to school.*
Does he ride a bike in the city?
--- *No, he rides a motorcycle in the city.*

cup

I drink milk in a cup. You drink tea in a white cup. She likes to drink tea in a little cup. He does not want to drink a cup of coffee today.

dollar

I have one dollar. You have two dollars. He has three dollars. She has four dollars. We have five dollars. They have only six dollars. We want more dollars. We want more money. I need to have seven, eight, nine or ten dollars.

Do you have two dollars?
---*Yes, I have two dollars. Why?*
I want to buy something to drink.
---*How much money do you need?*
I have one dollar. I need two more dollars.
--- *I will give you two dollars.*

to give

I	give
you	give
he	gives
she	gives
it	gives
we	give
you	give
they	give

food
apple
rice
juice
coffee
tea
money
ball
ride

I give a banana to my brother. You give a dollar to your sister. He gives some bread to the baby. She gives a ball to the dog. We give some grass to the cow. They give some rice to the children.

Can you give me some money?
--- *No, I do not have any money to give.*
Did you give water to the dog today?
--- *No, I did not give water to the dog. I did see the dog, and I did play with the dog, but I did not give water to the dog. I did give food to our dog, but I did not give water to our dog to drink.*
Will you give water to your cat?

--- Yes, I will give water to my cat. I like my cat. I want to give water to our cat and our dog. I like our cat and our dog. I like our animals.
Our baby brother likes to play with a ball. Will you give a ball to the baby so the baby can play with the ball?
---Yes, I like our baby brother. I will give a ball to our little baby brother.
What will you give to your little sister?
--- I will give a ball to my little sister also. She likes to play with a ball too.

doctor

A doctor helps people. I will go to a doctor tomorrow. I do not like to go to a doctor, but I have pain in my arm. You have pain in your leg. He has pain in his stomach. She has pain in her head. She has a headache. I have pain in my foot. My foot hurts.

Do you want to go to a doctor?
--- *No, I do not want to go to a doctor, but I have much pain. I will go tomorrow.*
Where does it hurt?
---*It hurts in my back. It also hurts here.*

_____
_____
_____
_____

to say

I	say
you	say
he	says
she	says
it	says
we	say
you	say
they	say

hi
hello
good morning
good night
no parking
good luck
what you like
the bus went (did go)

_____

_____

_____

_____

_____

The Story of the Little Chick

A little chicken is a chick. One day a little chick wanted *(did want)* some food. The little chick had *(did have)* a mother and a father. The little chick said *(did say)*, "I want some food." His mother said, "You can eat some grain." The little chick said, "I do not like to eat grain, I want other food. I will go. I will find some good food to eat."

The little chick went *(did go)*. He looked and he looked for some good food. He saw *(did see)* some apples. He ate *(did eat)* one apple. It was a good apple. Then he saw a banana. He ate a little of the banana, but he did not like the banana.

The little chick walked *(did walk)* and walked. He saw some corn. The little chick ate the corn. The corn was good. The little chick liked the corn.

The little chick walked and walked again. He saw a cow. The little chick spoke *(did speak)* to the cow. The little chick said, "What do you like to eat?" The cow said, " I like to eat grass and corn and grain." Then the little chick said, "What do you like to drink?" The cow said, "I like to drink water."

The little chick ate some grass, but he did not like to eat grass. The chick drank *(did drink)* some water. He liked to drink the water.

The little chick walked and walked. He saw a cat. The chick said to the cat, "What do you like to drink?" The cat said, " I like to drink milk. The cow gives me milk to drink." Then the chick said, "What do you like to eat?" The cat looked at the chick. The cat was hungry. The cat said, " I like to eat birds. Are you a bird? The little chick said, "No I am not a bird. I am a little chick." The cat looked at the chick again and said. "You look like a bird. I am hungry. Can I eat you?" No, no, said the chick.

The little chick wanted to go home. He wanted to see his mother and his father. The little chick went *(did go)* to his home very fast. His mother said. "Little chick, little chick, where did you go? We looked and we looked but we did not see you. Where did you go?"

The little chick said, " I went to look for some good food. I saw an apple and a banana. I saw a cow. The cow said he eats grass and corn and grain. I ate *(did eat)* some grass and some corn. I liked the corn and I liked the grain, but I did not like the grass. Then I saw a cat. The cat drinks milk. I did not drink milk. The cat said she likes to eat birds. She said I looked like a bird. I did not like what the cat said. The cat wanted to eat me. I went home very fast.

The mother and the father chicken were very happy to have their little chick at their house again.

to ask

I	ask
you	ask
he	asks
she	asks
it	asks
we	ask
you	ask
they	ask

a question
for help
my brother for some money
for directions
where to find something
when the store opens
how much does it cost
why he did that

I ask. you ask, he asks, she asks, John asks, we ask, you ask, they ask.

I ask my mother to help me find my book. You can ask someone where to buy good shoes. He asks his father to play with a ball. She likes to ask for help at the store. We ask what time the bus goes to the city. Yesterday he asked his brother for some money. Tomorrow they will ask for a ride to the city in his car.

What did you ask your sister ?
   --- I asked her for a banana.
Why don't you ask for help?
   --- I don't know how to ask questions.
Will you ask your brother to help?
   --- Yes, I will ask him tomorrow.

to cost

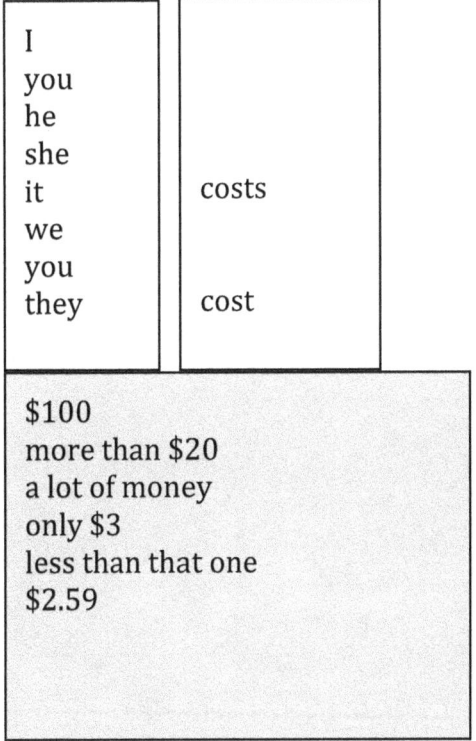

An apple costs $1. Bananas cost $4. Cars cost a lot of money.

How much do the apples cost?
--- *They cost one dollar.*
How much do the bananas cost?
--- *They cost four dollars.*
How much do cars cost?
--- *They cost a lot of money. They cost thousands of dollars.*
How much does that yellow car cost?

--- It costs ten thousand dollars.

The Story of the Red Car

One day a man went *(did go)* to the city to buy a car. He looked at a white car. He looked at a red car. He looked at a black car. The man liked the black car. The man wanted to buy the black car, but the black car was very expensive. The man did not have much money. He had *(did have)* very little money, so he went home. He did not buy the car that day.

That night the man spoke (did speak) to his wife. He said he wanted to buy the black car. His wife asked him how much the black car costs. He said it costs three thousand, five hundred dollars ($3500). She asked how much the red car costs. The man said the red car costs two thousand, four hundred dollars ($2400). His wife asked how much the white car costs. The man said the white car costs one thousand, two hundred dollars. ($1200).

The next day the man's wife gave *(did give)* him some food to eat for breakfast. She gave him some eggs and some bread to eat. The man ate *(did eat)* the eggs and the bread. She gave him some milk to drink. He drank *(did drink)* the milk. Then she said *(did say)*, "I like the white car. I want you to buy the white car today." The man looked at his wife. He said he liked the black car. He said, "I want to buy the black car today." His wife did not say anything. She said nothing. She looked at her husband. Then she said, "We can buy the white car, or we can buy the red car, but we can not buy the black car. The black car costs too much money. We do not have enough money to buy the black car. If we buy the black car we will not have enough money to buy a ball for the children to play. We will not have enough money to buy clothes for the baby. We will not have enough money to go to the store. We will not have enough money in the bank."

    The man looked at his wife. He smiled and said, "I like the red car. We will buy the red car." His wife smiled and said, "Yes, we will buy the red car." Then the man and the wife were happy. That day they went to the bank and they asked for two thousand dollars. They went to the city and they bought (did buy) the red car. They drove (did drive) to their house in their new red car.

to smile

I	smile
you	smile
he	smiles
she	smiles
it	smiles
we	smile
you	smile
they	smile

when I see a baby
every morning
at her
at him
too
to see the food
when you eat
when they drink juice

to work

I	work
you	work
he	works
she	works
it	works
we	work
you	work
they	work

at a store
for your boss
in a garage
in a restaurant
on the farm
every day
to get money
fast

I work to buy bananas. You work at a store. He works to have money. John works at a hotel. That is his job. My dog does not work. My cat does not work. It does not have a job. We like to work in our garden. They work in the garden to grow carrots and potatoes.

Do you work?
    --- *Yes, I work every day.*
Where do you work?
    --- *I work at a store in the city.*
What do you do at the store?
    --- *I sell food to people.*
What kind of food do people buy?
    --- *They buy eggs, bread, cheese, carrots, potatoes and milk.*
Do you like to work in the store?
--- *Yes, I like to work in the store. I need money. I buy food for my family with the money they give to me at the store.*
Do you work in your house?
    --- *Yes, I work in my house every day.*
What work do you do in your house?
    --- *I cook. I clean. I work in my garden.*

to say ... to grow

I	say
you	say
he	says
she	grows
John	grows
we	say
you	say
they	grow

hello to my wife
good afternoon
it is time to go
a good garden
apples on his farm
we like apples
you want to see a doctor
potatoes in their garden

What did the doctor say?
--- *She said I need to eat more vegetables.*
When did she say that?
--- *She said that when I saw her last week.*
Why did she say that?
--- *She wants me to eat good food everyday.*
Will you do what she says?
--- *Yes, I will do what she says. I want to be happy. I want to eat good food. I want to be strong. I do not want to be weak and sad. I will eat more vegetables.*

What do you grow in your garden?
We grow corn, peas, carrots and potatoes.

to cook ... to clean

I	cook
you	clean
he	cooks
she	cleans
John	cooks
we	clean
you	cook
they	clean

food for my children
the house everyday
food at a restaurant
houses for people
rice on Sunday
our car on Saturday
fish on Friday
their clothes on Wednesday

I cook food for my children. You like to clean your house. He does not like to clean the car. She cleans her clothes on Tuesday. Mary cooks rice and carrots for her family. We clean our house on Saturday.

Do you like to cook?
--- *Yes, I like to cook.*
Do you like to clean?
--- *No, I do not like to clean, but I like to have a clean house, so I clean my house everyday.*

Does your husband help clean the house?
--- *Yes, he is a good husband he helps to cook and he helps to clean. He works good and fast.*

The Story of the Family that Works

One day a family went (did go) to visit friends. They said (did say), "hello. How are you today?"

The friends said, "We are happy today."

Then the family asked, "Why are you happy?"

The friends said, "we are happy, because we have a good garden. Every day we work in our garden. We have many good things in our garden. Do you want to see our garden."

The family said, "Yes, we want to see your garden. Where is your garden?"

The friends said, "Our garden is behind our house. You can see our garden now. We will go behind our house to see our garden"

The family said, "Yes, we will go with you. We want to see it."

The family and the friends walked behind the house. There they saw (did see) a good, big, green garden. In the garden they saw carrots, potatoes, corn, onions, and peas.

The family asked, "Do you like to work in your garden?"

The friends said, "No, we do not all like to work in the garden. Mother likes to work in the garden. Father likes to work in the garden. But, brother and sister do not like to work in the garden. They like to play. They play with a ball. They play with the dog. They play with the cat, but they do not like to work in the garden.

    The family asked, "Do the children like to eat?"

The friends said, "Oh yes, they like to eat the carrots. They like to eat the peas. They like to eat the potatoes. They work in the garden not because they like to work. They work in the garden because they like to eat!"

    Everyone laughed, and laughed. The family had a good visit then they went to their house. At their house they looked behind their house and they said, "This is a good place for a garden. We will have a garden here too. We will work in the garden. Then we will eat food from our garden.

And they did.

to start ... to stop

I	start
you	stop
he	starts
she	stops
the bus	stops
we	start
you	stop
they	start

to read a book
work at five o'clock
a new job on Monday
at the store to buy food
in front of my house
school next week
the children at play
to work fast

I start a new job next week. You will start on Thursday. He starts to eat then he wants to play. She starts to sleep in the afternoon. The bus starts at six o'clock and stops at eleven o'clock. We start to play baseball in the morning. They want to start at eight o'clock on Saturday.

When did you start your new job?
--- *I started on Monday. I like my work.*

Does this bus stop at the store?
--- *No, it stops before the store. You will walk a little, then you will see the store.*
Does your car start in the morning?
--- *Yes my car does start on a good morning, but my car does not start on a bad morning.*
Do you want to speak English or do you want to stop?
--- *I want to speak English. I do not want to stop. I want to speak more and more everyday.*

to learn ... to understand

I	learn	to speak English
you	learn	with me
he	learns	very fast
she	understands	very well
it	understands	also
we	understand	the words in this book
you	learn	new words everyday
they	understand	the words I say

I like to learn new words in English. The words in this book are easy to understand. He wants to learn more words. She wants to learn more words too. The dog understands what I want him to do. The dog learns fast. The cow learns slowly. We learn fast. They learn slowly. We will help them learn so they can understand the words we say. They need to buy food, so they need to learn the words they need to buy food when they go to the store.

The Story of the Bus and the Car

One day a man wanted to go to work. He needed to go to his job very fast. He went (did go) to the bus stop and he waited for the bus. He did not see the bus. He waited again. He did not see the bus again. Then the man said. "I have a job. I need to go to work now."

The man saw a car. The man saw his friend in the car. The man said, "Can I ride in your car to my work?" His friend said, "Yes, you can ride in my car. I will drive to your work. You can go to your job with me. We will go now to your work.

Then the car stopped. The friend said, "Oh no. My car stopped." The man asked his friend why his car stopped. The friend said he did not understand why his car stopped. The man asked, "Is this a bad car?" His friend said, "No, this is a good car. I do not understand why my car will not go. What will we do now?"

The man looked. He saw a bus. He said, "I see the bus. We will go on the bus. You will go on the bus with me." So, the two men went out of the car and started to walk to the bus stop. They went on the bus. The bus went to the city. The man asked his friend where he wanted to go off the bus. His friend said he wanted to go off the bus at a car garage. He wanted to speak to the people in the car garage. He wanted to learn why his car stopped. The man said that he worked near a garage. They said, "We will go off the bus and we will speak with the people in the garage."

The bus stopped and the two men went off the bus. They walked to the garage. They said to the people in the garage that the friend's car stopped. They said they did not understand why the car stopped.

The people in the garage said that they needed to see the car to understand why the car stopped. They wanted the friend to drive the car to the garage for them to see the car and learn why the car stopped. The man looked at his friend. The friend looked at the man, then the two men looked at the people in the garage. Then they said, "We can not drive the car to the garage so you can see the car because the car will not go. The car stopped and the car will not start again.

The people in the garage laughed. Now they understood (did understand). You can not drive your car to our garage because your car will not go. They said, "One of our men will go drive one of our cars with you to see your car. Then we will learn why your car will not go. And they did.

to know ... to remember

I	know	many English words
you	remember	all the stories
he	knows	how to cook rice
she	remembers	his name
Mary	knows	where to buy food
we	remember	where the bus stops
you	know	what food they like
they	remember	that friend

Do you know how to cook rice?
--- *Yes, I know how to cook rice.*
Do you remember his name?
--- *No, I do not remember his name.*
Does she know more English words than you?
--- *Yes, she knows many English words. I only know a little English.*
Will you remember to go to the bank tomorrow?
--- *Yes, I will remember. I will not forget.*

to talk ... to listen

I	talk	with my friends
you	listen	to the stories
he	talks	on the phone
she	listens	to her friend
John	talks	to the people
we	listen	to the children
you	talk	to them
they	listen	at school

Did you talk to your friend today?
---Yes, I talked to her this morning. Every thing is fine and good. She will talk to me again this afternoon.
Do you listen to the baby at night?
--- Yes, I listen to the baby because the baby does not sleep well at night. The baby wants to eat food. But I do not want to give the baby food at night. I want the baby to sleep more.
Does your baby talk?
--- No, our baby is too little. She does not talk now. She will start to talk in three or four months.
Do the children listen in school?
---Yes, the children listen in school. They like school. They like to listen in school so they learn more and more. I am happy when the children

listen in school. I am also happy when the children listen to me in our house.

The Story of the Fish that Listened

One day a small fish said (did say)to his mother and his father. "I do not like this little water. I want to go in a big water. This water is too small."

His mother and his father said. "This water is our house. We like this little water. This is a good place. You will be happy here in this water. But the fish did not listen. He wanted to go to an other place. He wanted to see a big big water.

One day the fish saw (did see) a little place where the water went (did go) out. He went out of the little water. That night he was in a big big water. He was very happy. He said, "I like this big water. I want to be in this big water everyday. I do not like the little water with my mother and father. I will be in this big water many days.

The next day a man went down to the big water. He was a hungry man. He wanted to have a fish. He wanted to eat a fish. The man knew (did know) how to find a fish. The man knew how to have a fish from the big water.

The next day the little fish was very hungry too. He wanted to eat some food. He looked and he looked for some food in the new water, but he did not see any food in the big water. Then he looked again. He saw something in the water. The man had (did have) something in the water for the fish to eat. The little fish started to eat the food. The food was good but something hurt the little fish. Something was not good. The little fish remembered that his mother and his father said not to eat man's food. He also remembered that his mother and father said that the little water was a good place. The little fish was sad. He was not happy. The little fish stopped. He did not eat any more of the new food that the man had for him in the water. The little fish wanted to listen to his mother. He wanted to listen to his father. The little fish wanted to find his house. He wanted to go to his house in the little water.

    The little fish looked and looked. He did not find the little water. The little fish looked and looked again. Then he saw the place where the little water was. Then the little fish was happy. The little fish went fast. He found his little water. He found his mother and he found his father. He found his sister and his brother too.

    That night they all had (did have) some good fish food to eat. They were a happy fish family again.

to try ... to make

I	try	to eat slowly
you	make	bread to eat
he	tries	to learn fast
she	makes	something to drink
the dog	tries	to find the ball
we	make	money at our work
you	try	to start the car
they	make	clothes for children

Do you make good money where you work?
--- Yes, I make good money, but I do not like my job. I want to find an other kind of work.
Have you tried to find other work?
--- Yes, I have tried to find other work but it is not easy to find work now. I will work for one or two years, then I will find a new kind of work.
What do they make where you work?
--- They make all kinds of good food where I work. They make bread and cheese. They also make good things to drink.
Do you work at a restaurant?
--- Yes, that is where I work now. I can make more money at another restaurant, but I will work at this restaurant for one or two more years. I am happy to have this work. I like to make money. I need to make a little more money before I can buy a car.

What kind of car do you want to buy?
---*I will try to buy a big car with enough places for my mother and father and the children. But maybe, I will have to be happy with a small car.*

to live

I	live	at 123 White Street
you	live	in a large house
he	lives	with his brother
she	lives	in a big city
it	lives	on a farm
we	live	out of the city
you	live	on a small street
they	live	in a brown house

to put

I	put	a banana on the table
you	put	the apple in the bag
he	puts	the baby in the bed
she	puts	the food on the table
it	puts	its head in the house
we	put	the ball in the bag
you	put	some money in the bank
they	put	the milk in the cup

same - different

These two bananas are the same:

These two bananas are different:

sun

Today we see the sun.
It is a sunny day. I like the sun. We will have some sunny days. The sun helps our garden to grow. We will have some good food from our garden if we have enough sun.

rain

Today we have rain. It is a rainy day. He likes the rain. We will have some rainy days and some sunny days. The rain also helps our garden to grow. We need rain and sun to grow good food in our garden. If we will have rain tomorrow, we will have sun the next day. Our dog does not like the rain. The dog wants to go in our house when it rains. I said to my brother that I do not like to have the dog go in the house, but my brother likes our dog very much and he says that the dog can go in the house if it wants to.

police

I see the police on my street. Did you see the police yesterday at the store? Why did he speak to the police?

problem

My friend had a problem, so he went to the police. The police spoke (did speak) with him. The police asked him what was the problem. He said the problem was with his friend's dog. The dog spoke (did speak) all night and he did not sleep well. He does not like animals. He does not like cats. He does not like dogs. He does not like cows or horses. He only likes people.

Now you can speak English with 380 words. You say and do many things with these words. We will see now some of the things you can say and do.

When you see and speak to people:
Hi. My name is David. I am from the city _____ . I have a family. I have a mother and a father. I have a wife. Her name is _____ . We have eight children. We have six sons and two daughters. We do not have a dog or a cat. There is no place in our house for a dog or a cat. We do not have a cow, but I did have a horse when I was a small boy. We have a garden behind our house. It is a nice garden. In our garden we have peas, carrots, corn and potatoes. We like to have sunny days play, but we need some rainy days for our garden to grow. Where do you live? How many people are in your family? Do you have a job? Do you have any animals at your house? What kind of car do you have? Is it a good car? How much did it cost? I like you car. I like your family. I like you. We will be good friends.

When you go to the store:

Hi. How are you today? I want to buy some food. I want to buy one of those and two of these. How much is that? How much does this cost? I like the other one. How much is it? Thank you. I will give you the money. Do I have enough money to buy that? I will see you tomorrow. Thanks.

When you go to school:
Hello. How are you? I am fine, thank you. Our children want to go to this school. Can our children go to your school? When does the school start? What time of day does the school start? When does it stop? What time do the children stop school and go to their house? How much does it cost to go to this school? How many children go to this school? Are the teachers in this school good teachers? We like this school. Our children will be happy in this school. Thank you. We will see you in three days.

When you go to the car garage:
Hello. We have a problem with our car. The car will not go on cold days. Can you help us? How much will it cost to make our car go? Can you do it for less money? When can you start to work on our car? Can you give us the car in three days? Thank you.

When you go to the doctor:
Hi. I have a problem. I have pain in my two legs. Some days I have pain in my stomach too. I do not know what to do. I do not sleep well at night. I can not work in the day. This is a big problem for me. My children need to go to school everyday and I need to help them go to school. I also need to go to work everyday. I have a good job, but I can not work when I have this pain in my head or in my arms or legs. Can you help me? What will I do? Do you want me to eat something? What do you want me to eat? How many times do I eat this everyday? Will I be good in two days? Will I be good in five days?
Will I give this pain or this problem to my children in my house? Will I give this problem to my husband? He has a good job. He needs to be strong and happy at his job. He needs to sleep well at night. Can you help us? Thank you.

When you go to the restaurant:
Hi. How are you? We are fine. Yes, we are hungry today. We know that you have good food here. Our friends said (did say) that you have a lot of good food. Do you have fish in this restaurant? What kind of fish do you have? I like meat, but she does not like meat. She likes vegetables. Do you have some good rice in this restaurant? We want to have some water

please. He wants to have some coffee. He likes his coffee to be black. She wants to have some milk and sugar in her coffee. I do not want to have coffee, thank you. I like juice. Do you have juice in this restaurant? I like apple juice. If you do not have apple juice I like orange juice. Do you have orange juice? I want to have a large cup of orange juice. The children want a small meal. Do you have small meals for children? He wants to have a cup of milk. She wants a cup of water. We want to have meal six. They want to have meal seven. This looks like a good meal. Do you like this meal? I will have that meal. How much does it cost? Thank you.

When you go on a bus:
Hi. How much does it cost to ride on this bus? Where does this bus go? Where does the bus stop? Does this bus go downtown? Does this bus go to the city _____? Does this bus go near a restaurant? Is this the right bus to go to _____ ? Or, is this the wrong bus? Does the bus cost the same on Sunday as on Monday, or is the cost different? Does the bus cost the same for children as for big people? What time does the bus stop here? When does the bus go here again? Will I see the bus from here? Thank you.

This book is English380

Also look for English760

www.youtube.com
and
www.payloadz.com

Dr. David Clyde Walters

380 wordlist:

food
an
apple
a
banana
two
bananas
three
I
you
eat
he
she
it
eats
butter
bread
cheese
corn
egg
fish
fruit
grain
and
pig
we
they
cow
meal
meat
oranges
vegetables
rice
wheat
sugar
do   does
yes
no

grass
together
family
dog
do not don't
does not doesn't
speak speaks spoke
have has had
buy buys bought
go goes went
walk walks walked
drive drives drove
drink drinks drank
juice
milk
water
coffee
want wants wanted
write writes wrote
word words
sentence
question
like likes liked
my mine
your yours
his his
her hers
our ours
your yours
their theirs
car
red
white
airplane
yellow
house
this
that
these
those
am

are
is
hungry
thirsty
fine
happy
sad
good
bad
small
large
a little
a lot
few
many
some
much
most
very
any
almost
all
nothing
something
anything
on
in
who
what
when
how
where
why
here
at
noon
day
because
cup
old
me

him
her
us
them
with
yesterday
today
tomorrow
fine
thank you
last
night
now
next
week
Monday
after
lunch
afternoon
did
year
ago
Friday
hot
cold
easy
past
difficult
morning
but
there
right
wrong
correct
incorrect
before
pencil
green
tea
Spanish
Portuguese

English
Nepali
German
also
Italian
Chinese
Japanese
Korean
Russian
French
animal
arm
weak
strong
little
big
short
long
too
as well
four
leg
people
one
head
under
neck
shoulders
from
between
chest
inside
heart
below
stomach
pants
foot feet
shoes
five
six
seven

eight
nine
horse horses
ten
baby babies
bag
ball
round
child children
boy
play
everyday
baseball
out
off
over
outside
beside
bed
family
sleep sleeps slept
tonight
well
go
downtown
school
work works worked
store
church
bank
bus
job
Sunday
wait waits waited
stop
doctor
office
hospital
forget forgets forgot
need needs needed
enough

until
or
mother
father
sister
brother
wife
son
daughter
husband
man
woman
girl
grandparents
clock
watch
time
o'clock
minute
bird
blue
brown
black
see sees saw
her
him
fast
look looks looked
book
city
ride rides rode
bike
motorcycle
cup
dollar
give gives gave
so
pain
headache
hurt hurts hurt
story stories

chick chicken
can
other
find finds found
again
ask asks asked
question
help
directions
open opens opened
cost
say says said
hi
hello
parking
luck
more
than
only
less
expensive
thousand
hundred
if
clothes
smile smiles smiled
boss
garage
restaurant
farm
garden
grow grows grew
carrot
potato
sell
kind
Saturday
Wednesday
Tuesday
Mary
visit visits visited

friend
things
behind
onions
peas
laugh laughs laughed
place
front
start starts started
eleven
new
Thursday
then
slow slowly
near
name
learn learns learned
understand understands
understood
know knows knew
remember remembers
remembered
talk talks talked
listen listens listened
phone
try tries tried
make makes made
maybe
live lives lived
put puts put
street
same
different
sun
rain
police
problem

www.ingramcontent.com/pod-product-compliance
Lightning Source LLC
Chambersburg PA
CBHW022305060426
42446CB00007BA/591